# The Day You Became A MOM

*Written & Illustrated By*

KATJA ROSS

PURITY IN PEARLS BOOKS
MARYLAND

*Printing by DiggyPod: Digital Printing on Demand at DiggyPod.com*

**THE DAY YOU BECAME A MOM**

Published by Purity in Pearls Books

ISBN # 978-0-692-10194-0

This book is dedicated to all of the wonderful MOMs in my life!
I love you all soooooooooo much!
XOXOXOXOXO's

*The day you became a mom...*

*you became as fierce as a lion.*
*You wanted to protect your baby*
*from this, new, world they'd arrived in.*

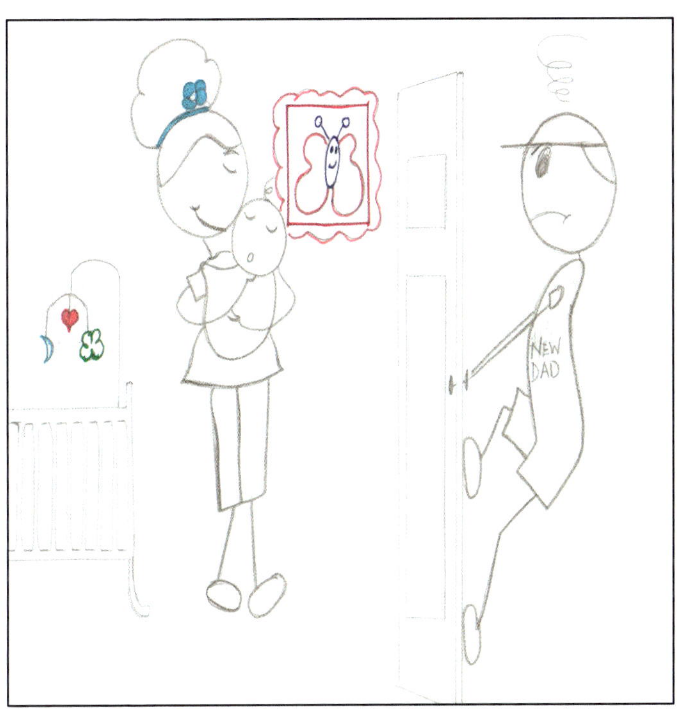
NEW
DAD

*The day you became a mom,
you became an expert in nutrition.
You even grew your own garden…*

and became an assistant pediatrician!

*__T__he day you became a mom,*
*you put away childish things.*
*Except, of course, those toys*
*that were "crucial" for joyful frolicking.*

*__T__he day you became a mom,
you became increasingly aware
that it was time to dump your sports car
for a vehicle with some real flare!*

***T**he day you became a mom,*
*You became a cheerleader and a teacher,*

*also, a friend, referee, coach,*
*Gourmet cook, chauffer and even a preacher!*

*The day you became a mom,*
*you may, even, have set some dreams aside,*
*so, that your children could accomplish theirs,*
*which filled you with joy and pride.*

*Though, sometimes, it wasn't so easy,*
*as there were many mountains to overcome.*

*The world became a better place*
*the day you became a mom!*

THE END